ASSORTED ARTICLES

DR. I. JOHNSON STEPHEN

To my family

Contents

Preface

This book is a collection of five original Research articles written and presented in various forums by Dr. I. Johnson Stephen from 2017 to 2021. All six articles are written with utmost care to project various aspects of the research arena. The titles of the six articles are as follows:

1. The Socio-Cultural Impact of the Suppressed Mind in D.H. Lawrence's *Lady Chatterley's Lover*
2. An "Inscape" journey from Freud to Lacan
3. The Function of the Mirror Stage as the Triple Formation of the 'I' in Constance Chatterley
4. God, the 'Obsessional Patient' – A Critique of John Milton's *Paradise Lost*
5. *Moral Aesthetics*: An Iconic Text in the Era of Post-truth – A Critique
6. 'Cultural Hegemony' as Hegemonic Culture in Atwood's *The Handmaid's Tale*

In all these articles, Literary Theories are applied to various literary works of art. In the first article, the researcher has applied the Psychoanalytical theory of Sigmund Freud. In the second article, Hermeneutics has been applied to relate both Freud and Lacanian Psychoanalysis. In the third article, Lacanian concept of Mirror Theory has been applied to the character namely Constance Chatterley from the novel titled *Lady Chatterley's Lover*. In the fourth article, Freudian analysis on his patient has been applied to the *Paradise Lost*. In the fifth article, the concept of Post-truth is applied in the book titled *Moral Aesthetics* to show the values of morality in the modern era. In the last article, Gramsci's term 'Cultural Hegemony' is applied in the novel *The Handmaid's Tale.*

The article titled "The Socio-Cultural Impact of the Suppressed Mind in D.H. Lawrence's *Lady Chatterley's Lover*" was presented at Arul Anandar College (Autonomous), Karumathur, in 2016 and it was published in the Seminar Proceedings with ISBN number. During this time, the author was pursuing his Doctoral Studies in Thiagarajar College, Madurai-09, as a Full-time Research Scholar. The character namely, Constance Chatterley, from D.H. Lawrence's novel *Lady Chatterley's Lover* is analysed.

The article titled "An "Inscape" journey from Freud to Lacan" was written in 2017 and was presented at A One Day National Conference on "Text as Con-Text: The Hermeneutic Circle Today" organised by St. Xavier's College, Palayamkottai. In this article, the theory of Hermeneutics is applied to show the relation between Sigmund Freud and Jacques Lacan.

The article titled "The Function of the Mirror Stage as the Triple Formation of the 'I' in Constance Chatterley" was published in 2017 at the TEJAS, a Research Journal (Online) run by Thiagarajar College, Madurai. During the publication of this paper, I was pursuing my Doctoral Studies under the guidance of Dr. M. Elangovan, Associate Professor, PG and Research Department of English, Thiagarajar College, Madurai – 09. The paper was corrected by Dr. M. Elangovan and Dr. V. Subathra Devi, the Head, PG and Research Department of English, Thiagarajar College, Madurai – 09, after the later's consent and permission it was published in the College Journal. This paper analyses the female protagonist namely Constance Chatterley of D. H. Lawrence's novel *Lady Chatterley's Lover* and she is analysed with Lacanian views on the Mirror Stage.

The article titled "God, the 'Obsessional Patient' – A Critique of John Milton's *Paradise Lost*" was published in ACJELL, a Journal run by The American College Madurai, in 2016. This article inquires God's mentality behind the banishment of both Adam and Eve from the Garden of Eden. It treats God as a Patient who has lot of emotional anger which forces him to hold such a position in the society. God has 'taboo sickness' in his mind. He creates Adam and Eve and gives control over everything in the Garden of Eden. But after eating the forbidden fruit from the tree of knowledge they are expelled from the Garden of Eden. God is the pioneer in the field establishing the concept of taboo in this world. Actually, the researcher borrows the concept 'taboo' from Sigmund Freud's seminal work Totem and Taboo. Taboo means something prohibited and sacred which is treated as an unusual thing in order to protect the moral norms in this world. The paper aims at showing both God and the first parents are the practioners of the tabooed concepts in the Garden of Eden.

The next article is titled as "'Cultural Hegemony' as Hegemonic Culture in Atwood's *The Handmaid's Tale*". This article was presented in December 2021 at 3rd RSRI Conference on Contemporaneity of Language and Literature in the Robotized Millenium in Arul Anandar College (Autonomous), Karumathur, Madurai District. The term *Hegemony,* isfrequentlyused in the works of Late and Neo-Marxist Philosophers, literally means domination of the ruling class over the culture, economy and *status quo* of those who are administrated. The Italian Marxist, Antonio Gramsci, uses the term *Hegemony* as the apparatus of the State to rule the subordinate class through certain dictating institutions; religion, schools, and media. Through unleashing the power over the subordinate class, the State accomplishes certain right wing policies. Gramsci asserts, in his *Prison Notebooks,* that "state should be understood not only as the apparatus of government, but also the "private" apparatus of "hegemony" or civil society" (261). The institutions regulate the 'consent' of the 'civil society' using violence and ideology over them, i.e. ruling class ideology. The Canadian futuristic novel *The Handmaid's Tale* tells the story of the usurpation of the American soil by the 'State' called the Republic of Gilead. The power of the State is expressed through the Republic of Gilead, which uses religion as a major repressive apparatus to educate the right wing tendencies. The ruling class in the novel is "essentially conservative in the sense that they [do] not tend to construct an organic passage from the other classes into their own, i.e. to enlarge their class sphere "technically" and ideologically" (*Prison Notebooks*, 260). Rather, it edifies the subordinate classes to be the victims. Women are treated as a "means of production" of children in this dystopian novel. The freedom of men and women is restricted; even there is no outlet for men's sensuality. The magazines and pornographic channels are forbidden in Gilead. This paper analyses this prevalent condition in the novel *The Handmaid's Tale* through 'Cultural Hegemony' of the Republic of Gilead. The novel is analysed from the perspective of the two seminal Marxist critics of the twentieth century, namely, Antonio Gramsci and Louis Althusser.

This book is the first original venture of the author.

Acknowledgements

I would like to extend my sincere gratitude to Dr. M. Elangovan, Associate Professor of English, Thiagarajar College, Madurai. Under his able guidance, all the articles in this book were written and presented.

I thank my wife Mrs V. Sumathy Johnson Stephen for helping me in typing and aligning the articles. I thank my family members for their continuous encouragement in my endeavours.

The Socio-Cultural Impact of the Suppressed Mind in D.H. Lawrence's "Lady Chatterley's Lover"

There are various factors which formulate the character of a man. As for as an individual is concerned, society and its culture determine an individual's character. So the individual and the society are inseparable. Culture also plays a vital role in the formation of an individual. Society has both good and evil things in it. But what an individual takes in is evil and not good. The evil and good qualities have been cultivated in this individual through the family members. Family is the first one to give both moral and evil qualities to society. The individual forms some good and bad things in him or her. These qualities are also determined by an individual's mind or psyche. So the human psyche is the product of both society and its culture.

The human psyche can be weighed through one particular factor which is psychoanalysis. When one says of psychology immediately Freud comes to mind. Freud, the father of psychoanalysis, the man who analyzed his patients' minds, introduced some analysis which is now called psychoanalysis. He dissected the human mind into three parts, the Id, Ego and Super-ego. The Id is the storehouse for the repressed thoughts of human beings. The Ego is the conscious level of human beings and the super-ego is the sub-conscious level of human beings.

This paper shows how far the mind is the result of the impact of social norms and cultural values. The unconscious mind is a "Pleasure Principle". It is the stock room for the repressed or suppressed actions of human beings. The role is taken over by the subconscious mind. It only resolves that one should do good or evil things in front of others. If the mind negotiates bad actions (rape, molestation, sexual intercourse in public etc.,) all these were restricted in society. So the desires have been suppressed and these desires have been sent to the human unconscious realm. When one suppresses those desires of the unconscious it becomes apparent in two different ways: the returning of the suppression and the expression of the suppression. These concealed desires must have an outlet in different forms. Freud revealed that unconscious desires find their expressions through dreams, jokes, and slips of the tongue.

D. H. Lawrence is a man of psychological expression, the poet, novelist, critic of the beginning of the twentieth century, and psychoanalyst to some extent. Readers of Lawrence consider him as 'fire'. One must have a keen understanding of Lawrence to understand the socio-cultural and its impact on an individual. F. R. Leavis says "not only is he [D. H. Lawrence] our last great writer; he is still the great writer of our phase of civilization" (Leavis).

Lawrencian characters are the victims of socio-culture. His writings are the epitome of socio-cultural impact. His novels portray the human predicament in the modern world. Many consider him a great novelist. *Lady Chatterley's Lover* highlights the protagonist's suppressed mind is the product of the socio-cultural impact.

Connie, as shortly known in the novel, has happened to lead an unhappy life with her husband, who has been severely wounded in the First World War. The second part of the novel focuses on how Connie makes an illicit relationship with Mellors. Connie, a girl of rich parents, had many flirtations with her German boyfriend. After the marriage with Clifford Chatterley, for two years the couple enjoys marital life to the core. But fate has a central role in marital life of Connie. She does not have a sexual relationship with her husband after he becomes paralyzed forever. Her life is apt for what has been said by Lawrence at the beginning of the novel:

"OURS is essentially a tragic age, so we refuse to take it tragically. The cataclysm has happened, we are among the ruins, and we start to build up new little habitats, to have a little hope. It is rather hard work: there is now no smooth road into the future: but we go around, or scramble over the obstacles. We've got to live, no matter how many skies have fallen" (*Lady Chatterley's Lover*, p. 1).

Connie's life becomes tragic but she refuses to accept it tragically. She is among the runs after her husband crippled forever. She starts to live her life with new little hopes. Her only hope is Mellors. But there is no smooth road to their life (Mellors and Connie).

Lacan's developed concept of "*Jouissance*", which means an extreme form of pleasure: ecstatic and orgasmic bliss a woman gets in bed, has been applied here. Connie in Chapter seven of the novel looks at her nude body in front of the mirror and concludes that her body needs to get pleasure, which in Lacan's words '*Jouissance*'. No woman attains this *jouissance* in bed with men. Similarly, Connie never attains this with her husband. When she sees her nudity her old desires (Connie's sexual relationship with her German boyfriend) reawaken the present desires (attains *jouissance*). This act is nothing but the return of the suppression that the researcher has said already. Her position is described as "Unjust! Unjust! The sense of deep physical injustice burned to her very soul" (LCL, 74).

Connie now seeks Mellors to enjoy sex. Now the expression of the suppressed desires begins to sprout. What obstruct Connie are society and the culture. Her mind keeps on suppressing the desire to get Mellors. Society does not accept this type of relationship. So the desires have been suppressed by society. When she visits Mellor's farm she happens to see the bare body of Mellors and her return of the unconscious fully revealed in her mind. This is called the return of the repressed.

As the researcher has said at the beginning of this paper, the unconscious is the "Pleasure Principle". Connie's unconscious desires seek their pleasure in the hands of Mellors. Mellors is the phallic object and has control over the female body. The return of the suppression of Connie's desires finds its pleasure in the expression of the suppression. Everything in this world is determined by society. The individual is resolved by the other. The deeds of an individual are not his or her character but they are the reflection of what an individual acquires from society.

Works Cited

1. Esthope, Antony. *The Unconscious*. Routledge: London, 1999. Print.
2. Lacan, Jacques. *Ecrits: A Selection*. Routledge Classics: London, 1989. Print.
3. Lawrence, D.H. *Lady Chatterley's Lover*. Penguin: Great Britain, 1997. Print.
4. Leavis, F. R. *D. H. Lawrence: Novelist*. Great Britain: Penguin Books, 1955. Print.
5. Malpas, Simon. Wake, Paul., ed. *The Routledge Companion to Critical Theory*. London and New York: Routledge, 2006. Print.

CHAPTER II

An "Inscape" journey from Freud to Lacan

Structuralistic critics consider a work of art as 'text' which designates a completely different meaning from the concept of a work of art. On the contrary, this school of theory originated from Post-Structuralism, which insists upon the concept of 'intertext'. This 'intertextuality' is one of the major concepts used in reconstructing a text. All "literary texts are woven out of other literary texts, ... in the more radical sense that every word, phrase or segment is a reworking of other writings... [so] all literature is intertextual." (Terry Eagleton, *Literary Theory: An Introduction*, 119). The researcher here takes up the deconstructing concept of intertextuality as a tool to relate both the Father of Psychology, namely Sigmund Freud and the charismatic thinker Lacan through Hermeneutics, which is an understanding of the process of understanding a text. The research statement of this paper insists on an 'inscape' journey from not Freud to Lacan but from Freudian texts to Lacanian texts. After a brief introduction to these two legends, the researcher will show how their texts come under the Hermeneutic circle.

The concept of intertextuality applies to the field of Psychoanalysis. Beginning his career as a research scholar in the field of Psychology, Freud investigated the minds of patients. He was inspired by the hypnotism of Charcot, under whom Freud studied, and introduced a kind of treatment in the field of Psychology. He is the founder of

Psychoanalysis, which was formulated for reading the mind of his patients only after he became a doctor. He introduces many concepts in the field of psychoanalysis. Some of his major concepts are the Id, Ego and Super-ego, the theory of interpreting Dreams, Infantile Sexuality, and the Oedipus complex.

Whatever Freud introduced was only for the field of Psychoanalysis. Like all other theories, Freudian theory slowly began to fade away. The development of American Neuroscience slowly began to erode Freudian principles. The man who established a new school of Psychoanalysis after his name is Jacques Lacan. He is one of the seminal thinkers of the Twentieth century France. He began his career as a trainee in the field of Psychoanalysis and began to set his strong foot among the intelligentsia of France. His concepts were a shocking threat to the traditional school of Psychoanalysis. As an influential thinker, he draws his inspiration from various fields such as Linguistics, Post-Structuralism, Surrealism, and Mathematics. Like Freud, Lacan also contributed major concepts to the field of Psychoanalysis. His theories such as the Mirror Phase, theories regarding Object, ideas regarding the three stages of life as Imaginary, Symbolic and Real, his emphasis on the Signifier, his concept of an eighteen-month child, and his insistence on the letter and speech shows that he is one of the seminal thinkers in the field of Psychoanalysis and Post-Structuralism.

Hermeneutics is considered to be a theory of interpreting any biblical exegesis. Later days it is defined as the understanding of the process of understanding a text. Similarly, Lacan's works in the field of Psychoanalysis are the understanding of Freudian understanding. If Freud is the founder of Psychoanalysis, Lacan is the developer of

Freudian ideologies and he has established himself as a milestone in this field. Lacan introduces Post-structuralism into Freudian ideologies.

Freud considered that a human being is acting upon only his unconscious mind. 'Id' is another name for the Unconscious mind. It is the reservoir of human 'drives' and 'desires'. This unconscious does not care about social norms rather it wants pleasure alone. So Freud called this mind a 'pleasure principle'. When the unusual thoughts of the Ego mind, in other words (*Écrits*) the conscious mind, is suppressed by society, the repressed thoughts are found in their place in the Unconscious mind. These thoughts have to find their outlet in one form or the other. Similarly, the dream is one of the forums through which a human unconscious feeling expresses itself. So Freud ultimately suggests that the dream is an expression of human unfulfilled desires. The dream can haphazardly narrate its story, since the desires in the unconscious mind, the storehouse, are not chronologically arranged. This idea led Freud to conclude that the dream is a rebus, a synonym for the puzzle, and it has no order in it a Psychoanalyst must let patients' unconscious mind find an outlet by 'talking' to them and this technique is called a 'talking cure'.

For many years this concept of unconsciousness held its controversial status. Many psychiatrists especially American Neuroscience begin to develop a skeptic notion regarding the Freudian conception. So slowly the Freudian ideologies begin to faint. But the new man from France came forward to take up the Freudian concepts and he put Freudian ideologies into a different perspective.

Lacan is a staunch follower of the Structuralist concept of a 'Sign' and develops his ideology regarding the 'Signifier' than the 'signified'. What Lacan rereads in Freud is his way of interpreting the human unconscious mind. Lacan acknowledges Freud as a discoverer of the term 'unconscious' mind. But, he in some respects said that Freud uses language to interpret dreams which plays a very important notion in the significance of the dream.

Lacan insists on the idea of Ferdinand de Saussure that a 'sign' is a combination of a 'signifier' and a 'signified'. But he goes to another extant that 'Signifier' has its priority over the 'signified'. He said that the "Unconscious is the whole structure of language." (*Écrits*, 163). Freud himself does not know his invention of the unconscious mind has this language structure.

Lacan gives a series of ideas about how the unconscious mind is structured like a language.

1. "Dream is like the parlour game" in which the audience has to guess some well-known sayings in a dumb show.
2. Unconscious is one of the several elements of a representation of the dream.
3. Dream uses speech.
4. Dream work follows the law of 'Signifier'.

According to Lacan, the very talking of the patient involves speech. If Freud says that unconscious desires involve talking and he in one way represents the importance of Language in the unconscious mind. Lacan had the texts of Freud as models and he interprets his dream process through the lens of Linguistics. If one wants to know Lacan completely one has to possess in-depth knowledge of Freudian texts.

According to the theory of Hermeneutics, Lacan when considering the subject of his self is a better understanding of the critical and psychological ideas regarding human beings. Lacan on the other hand rethinks Freud and his concepts. But he reconstructs Freud and his texts. In a post-structuralist view, a text reconstructs itself. Similarly, Lacan is the intertext of Freud and modern Psychoanalysis. His texts are produced out of another context, (Freudian context). So there is a kind of inter-textual framework between Freud and Lacan. Thus both texts of Freud and Lacan come under the Hermeneutic circle. If the Lacanian texts are taken up for future analysis, once again his texts will metamorphose themselves and become a forerunner to produce another context with a Hermeneutic circle which is in a circulation mode and deconstructive process which has a kind of eternal negation of its existence.

Works Cited

1. Eagleton, Terry. *Literary Theory: An Introduction.* London: Blackwell Publishers; 1983. Print.
2. Lacan, Jacques. *Écrits: A Selection.* Routledge Classics; London: 1989. Print.

CHAPTER III

The Function of the Mirror Stage as the Triple Formation of the 'I' in Constance Chatterley in D.H. Lawrence's "Lady Chatterley's Lover"

It is quite a big task to know the act of intelligence. Some of the people are judged by only their intelligence and the remaining by their wisdom. Is the act of intelligence an inherent quality? The process of finding out the answer for this question remains a crucial one. People say that it is an inborn quality. But the thing is different. The act of intelligence is not an inherent quality. It is achieved by a human being only by looking at others by which he/she may distinguish himself/herself from other objects. If intelligence is an acquired quality, rather than inborn, when and whereby it is acquired and in what way it is acquired? At which period of time does a human being can cultivate the art of intelligence?

Intelligence is an art. Each and every human being inherits this inborn quality, as considered by many, in the age of just eighteen months. It is a great threat to the traditional believes of so many subjects (human beings, as treated by Psychoanalysis). This idea is proved by a generous and a charismatic leader of the Psychoanalysis namely Jacques Lacan. He, in 1936, introduced a concept called 'Mirror Stage' in one of his seminars titled "Mirror Stage as the Formation and the Function of the 'I' as revealed in the Psychoanalystic Experience". In the 'Mirror stage',

"The child, at an age of when he is for a time however short, outdone by the chimpanzee in instrumental intelligence, can nevertheless already recognise as such his own image in a mirror. This recognition is indicated in the illuminative mimicry of the Aha-Ertebnis, ... an essential stage of the act of intelligence." (P-1, Lacan *Écrits*).

How far does the 'Mirror Stage' become an act of intelligence in the case of a child?

At the stage of infancy a child, however it is a little one, looks at the mirror, either by itself or forced by others, comes across a series of gestures and images of its surroundings. It experiences the relationship between the movements of its body and the reflection of the environment. It gets into a kind of confused state between the image and the reflection. Now the child understands the discrimination between it and the replica of the reality though it lacks the 'signs' this act takes place 'from the age six months'.

One thing remains worthwhile in the act of looking at mirror that is 'gaze'. The term 'gaze' is nothing but a slight look on something. This gaze brings an instantaneous image in the child about it. This activity of the child remains one of the landmarks in its life. It leads to the libidinal dynamism. On the whole, the mirror stage acts as an identification of the 'self' and 'Other'. An act of metamorphosis takes place in the subject about the image and the duplicity of the reality. One has to note a significant thing in this stage that is when an infant gets into this metamorphosis, 'I' becomes a primordial form, before it gets into a symbolic matrix or objectified by the dialectical system or identification with the 'Other'. This metamorphosis causes the act of intelligence of an infant as a subject.

What becomes an intellectual capacity of a child 'I', the condition of the metamorphosis is its 'identification with the other party'. This becomes an epitome of the intelligentsia of an infant in its infantile stage. The role of stimulating an infant to identify this 'I' which becomes the 'Ideal-I', is done by a 'motor'. So the 'motor' capacity of the child registers the identification of the 'I' in the 'register' of a child. The 'self' of the child is attributed or taught by the 'Other'(s) of the family or society. When the child is born in this world, its mind is nothing but a 'Tabula Rasa' (in Greek it means a clean slate). The others or the exteriority of an infant with its dialectic of identification begins to scribble the slate.

What remains a crucial issue in the child during the 'mirror phase' is its discrimination of the real and the fragment. Slowly the child recognises him as a symbol or the 'Signifier'. The specular image of the child becomes 'the meaning' or the 'signified'. Thus the mirror phase serves a twin role in the child: one is 'the Ideal I' and the other is the 'symbolic function' around him.

The binary opposition 'self' (I) x 'Other' becomes a central issue in the life of a child. Thus testing itself with the understanding of this binary opposition, a child begins to set its foot on life. Later it has been objectified by the language dynamism. Finally

"the mirror-stage would seem to be the threshold of the visible world, if we go by the mirror disposition that the *imago* of the one's own body presents in hallucinations or dreams, whether it concerns its individual features, or even its infirmities, or its object – projections; or if we observe the role of the mirror apparatus in the appearances of the *double*, in which psychical realities, however heterogeneous, are manifested" (3).

By looking at the mirror, the desire is kindled in a child. The mirror disposition creates a spatial capitation before the child is united with the social dialectic. The specular 'I' connects the 'I' to the social 'I', which structures the human knowledge through creating desires. The man becomes superior to the animal in knowledge. He gets autonomy in knowledge. But he becomes the victim of the vicious psychic reality of the world.

What is the outcome of the 'mirror phase'?

The ultimate factor or impact is created by 'mirror phase' is on the human beings is the 'specific prematurity of birth' in man. So the kind of individualistic attitude is created in the psyche of the child. The mirror stage becomes a drama which manufactures the subject and creates a temporal dialectic through which the subject's entire mental development has been structured. When the dialectic stage begins there ends the mirror stage and the man begins to encounter three things in Oedipus Complex:

1. The desire of the 'Other'
2. The Instinctual Thrust
3. The natural maturation of him is depended upon the cultural mediation.

The 'Oedipus Complex' is the term introduced by Sigmund Freud and it was taken from the Greek play titled *Oedipus, the Rex*, written by Sophocles ('Rex' means King). Oedipus married his own mother. Mother is seen as a sexual object by her own son, which is considered to be the Oedipus complex.

The human being for the first time begins to think that he is a sexual object at 'mirror stage'. The 'mirror stage' introduces two important knots,

1. Oedipus complex
2. Narcissistic ideology

When one looks at the mirror disposition one undergoes the Narcissistic love (self-love) by which he/she loves his/her own body. The 'mirror stage' not only displays the Narcissistic love but also it re-forms the dead 'I' which is oppressed by the social 'I'. So the Narcissism plays a vital role for the re-formation of the 'self'.

Every human being is the subject of this tragic world. When havoc summons, the human beings must obey and every one of us is not excluded from Narcissistic ideologies. People look at the mirror, where they beautify themselves with lots of cosmetics. People not only regenerate their appearance but also give importance to the physical sensuality.

So, the mirror disposition plays an important role in the lives of human beings. The mirror is the only object which shows the specular motions of the human peculiarity. The application of the mirror disposition is prevalent in the society. It becomes a part and parcel of human life. Literature is one of the major areas to project life as it is. It gives some remedies for the people who are disturbed by so many ruins in their lives. The title of this research paper, "The Function of the Mirror Stage as the Triple Formation of the 'I' in Constance Chatterley", indicates the application of 'mirror stage' in Lawrencian character namely, Constance Chatterley in his novel named *Lady Chatterley's Lover.*

D.H. Lawrence is one among the few major contributors of the novelistic form and he is the most prolific writer of the early Twentieth century. He is still considered to be the most notorious man by people. The researcher of this article focuses one of Lawrence's most notorious characters among all of his novels namely Constance Chatterley. She is the lady protagonist of the novel *Lady Chatterley's Lover*. Her story is set during the World War I. The novel was published in 1928. It was banned in Great Britain for its sexual content. But this novel is considered to be an unsurpassed in the field of celebrating sexual love which gives a new dimension and frankness to the body.

When one looks at the story of Constance Chatterley one blames her as a prostitute. But one cannot blame her if one understands the tragic events in her life. The Twenty three years old Constance marries a man who is well - built. The couple enjoys their honeymoon for a month. But the World War I has brought the ceiling down over her head. She has to spend her life with her husband, who is paralysed forever in his life. As a result Connie, as shortly known, has had an affair with Mellors, the game keeper.

The predicament of female is just the same in every nation. She has to absolutely a dependent on her husband for everything, to get financial support or to get sex thing. Similarly, Connie is fully dependent on her husband Clifford. But usually a female is helpless when she does not have sex with her husband, which is a basic thing for every man and woman. By marrying a woman, man wants to assert his superiority over her. But females somehow manage their problems. Connie in this novel is projected in such a way to subside her sensual affections and feelings inside her. Connie does not have a smooth road to the future, since the cataclysm has happened. But she strives for the visionary life to her. She and her 'Ideal − I' is submerged in the cataclysm of her life. She becomes the victim of the vicious circle of men.

As per the psychical development of a human being, Connie must have undergone the 'mirror phase' in her age of eighteen months. The series of reflective images of her surroundings must have made her or taught her the function of the 'I'. With the help of this first formulation of the 'I', Connie must have had undergone the stage of 'Electra complex', a daughter having a kind of husbandly love towards her father. The 'Others' of her family decides the desire of Connie. The desire of the Others of Connie directs her sexual feelings towards any one of the gentlemen of her surroundings, by whom she might have had the fulfillment of her sexual desires. The female 'I' has become the subject which subjugates the men only in an intercourse. Similarly, Connie also subjugates Clifford for nearly one or two months on her bed. The 'I' of Connie becomes the 'I'ness in the hands of Clifford, her husband. The 'I'ness of Connie let itself become the diminishing factor in the hands of 'Other' with 'O' in capital. This becomes the first formation of the 'I' in 'mirror phase'.

Constance's life is an embodiment of the triple formation of the 'I' or 'self' by 'others'. After becoming a scapegoat in the hands of self-estimated circle of men, Connie's second awakening of the 'I' is formulated. She is slowly becoming one with the cataclysm of her life. Among the vicious circle of men, who are 'others' to Connie, one of the 'Other' among the 'others' re-constructs the subjugated 'I' of Connie, but not fully. The 'self'ness of Connie wants to dedicate herself fully to her paralysed husband. So she willingly suspend her 'I'ness and becomes the subject of the Subject. But the subjectness (Connie) of the subject (Clifford) is taken away by the 'Other' not among the circle of men, but by the gamekeeper Mellors.

Usually, the body alone cannot hide anything from what has been called so far as immorality. When one controls the mind, one cannot control one's body, the urge of the body of the 'self' goes beyond the mind. One's 'I'ness is proved only through his / her body. Similarly, the dead 'I' of Connie is stimulated to form itself fully once again by the body of Mellors' (Other). The washing scene of the 'Other' (Mellors) becomes

"a visionary experience: it had hit her (Connie 'I') in the middle of the body. She saw the clumsy breaches slipping down over the pure, delicate, white loins, the bones showing a little, and the sense of aloneness, of a creature purely alone, overwhelmed her. Perfect, white, solitary nudity of a creature that lives alone, and inwardly alone. ... a lambency, the warm, white flame of a single life, evealing itself in contours that one might touch: a body!" (LCL -69)

The scene makes her think the 'positionality' of the position of Connie, the subject. It seizes the dedication of Connie's 'self' to the 'Other' (her husband Clifford) into reality, by which this visionary experience of Connie kindles the subjugated 'I'ness of Connie again is kindled to the second formation and the function of it. In such a way, the second formation of the 'I'ness of Connie gives its breath to the dead or the lost "I" of her.

Here the 'I' ness of Connie comes under the Lacanian formation of the 'mirror stage', but it goes beyond the ideas of Lacan. Anyhow the 'Other' becomes an active function in the passive 'I' or 'self'. But stimulated by the active 'Other', the 'I' of Connie goes for the third formation of the 'I' in the mirror disposition.

The elated 'self' of Connie in her sitting room takes away all her cloths and gets ready for the Narcissistic experience. By which act, Connie's desires become the desires of the Narcissus. The 'self' jubilant attitude of Connie becomes the 'I' of the 'Other'. So here Lacan's interpretation of the 'mirror phase' is reconstructed by the 'self' of Connie. If according to Lacan the 'mirror phase' becomes the threshold of the visible world, the second 'I'ness of Connie remains the 'imago of one's own body' and becomes the second entry or door to the world of adult sex. The third formation of the 'I'ness of Connie (before the mirror) remains the triple formation of the 'I' which proves the superiority and the everlasting 'I' in every subject.

So what remains the important factor is that the 'I' is determined by the 'I'ness of the 'Other'(s). The whole of the human beings must remember one thing that the body alone can create cause to its various desires. These desires are not formed by the 'self' or 'I' but by the 'Other'. Thus, Connie becomes an experiment of the triple formation of the 'I', in such a way it reconstructs itself.

Works Cited

1. Evans, Dylan. *An Introductory Dictionary of Lacanian Psychoanalysis*. London and New York: Routledge, 1996. Print.
2. Lacan, Jacques. Écrits: A selection. Trans. Alan Sheriden. London and New York: Routledge, Classics, 1977. Print.
3. Lawrence, D. H. *Lady Chatterley's Lover*. Great Britain: Penguin Popular Classics, 1997. Print.
4. Sigmund, Freud. *The Ego and the Id*. USA: Pascps, 2010. Print.

God, the Obsessional Patient – A Critique of John Milton's "Paradise Lost"

The present paper probes God in the perception of the Psychoanalytical Criticism. The title of the paper enlightens and cares for God as Patient, who is affected by unhealthy obsession or controlled by the evil spirits without the possession. One should not be misled by the statement of this research article since it inquires the concept of God. The researcher, just, applies the psychoanalytical criticism of Freudian school on God to disclose his totemic and tabooed concepts. The main source of this article is a 'magnum opus' in English Literature namely, the *Paradise Lost* and one of the greatest and thought provoking piece of books – namely, *Totem and Taboo*, in the field of Psychoanalytical criticism.

Freud's book *Totem and Taboo* is one of the ground-breaking works of Psychoanalysis. It is the fullest exploration of his famous themes, such as, family, society and religion. The researcher while writing this article does not stand neither on the side of religion nor on the secular side, rather holds the neutral position to note down the social role played by God, while punishing both Adam and Eve. In this article one can witness the Satanic influence on God. Since the researcher has touched the Christian concept of theology, let no other Indian religion may claimthe producer as an accuser. But a real thinker can understand the extreme role played by the religious system and uncodified moral laws behind the punishment of God on the first parents.

Psychoanalytical field believes that there is a kind of prohibition which causes a man or woman to become a patient. A patient, who is not only has to have diseases but also inherits the mental illness which is the result of the prohibitions or banishment of some desires. What is prohibited here or banned? Usually every civilisation and culture has its strong beginning from religion and moral consciousness. This religious attitude is not inseparable from the civilisation of one particular group of people. The same people lay down certain moral codes to be followed in their own race. If anyone trespasses the code written by those race of people he will be treated as an untouchable. The untouchability finds its opening in the minds of the other people who belong to the same race of people. So here the untouchability becomes the prohibition.

The word 'taboo' aptly suits to the concept of prohibition or banishment. Taboo is a Polynesian word as it is said by Freud in *Totem and Taboo*. The word taboo is untranslatable one, to which one cannot give the exact meaning. But one can define what is meant by taboo? Taboo is a kind of practice practised by every society, at certain rate of judgment, as something or some activities are done against it, which are usually banned.

Though 'taboo' is untranslatable, Sigmund Freud leads the readers to two contrary directions while attributing meaning to the signifier 'taboo' in *Totem and Taboo*. 'Taboo' has two meanings; such as something which is 'Sacred' and the other is 'forbidden', the former leaves the positive insight while the later indicates the negative. Taboo is something that is aloof for human beings. The nature of the taboo is expressed only in the prohibitions and restraints in the society. But one has to know that Freud's suggestion that the concept of Taboo is not based on the moral prohibitions. Some say that Taboo is the "oldest human unwritten code of laws" and "older than Gods" (Wundt). So the concept taboo is of unknown in origin.

Psycho-analytical examination examines the nature of the taboo which includes

i. the sacred or unclean,
ii. the kind of prohibition which results from the character and
iii. the sanctity which results from a violation of the prohibition (*Totem and Taboo*, 22).

Psycho-analytical field analyses that taboo is committed either 'indirect or natural' possession of the demonic power in a person or it is taught by other person. A wife even can influence her husband to commit taboo or vice-versa. This ideological attribution of taboo can be applied to the chief characters in the *Paradise Lost*, namely Adam and Eve. Even to some extent by God himself.

The objectives of 'taboo' are

a. to protect important persons or things such as, chief activities in the society and something which is given much more importance – 'Forbidden fruit' in the *Paradise Lost*.
b. to preserve the feeble persons from the powerful influences – temptation of Eve by Satan.
c. the guarding of the sexual impulses and functions – Understanding the self in *Paradise Lost*.

Freud has systematically observed the punishment for violating taboo in his *Totem and Taboo*. So, the punishment among the ancient people was "no doubt originally left to an internal, automatic agency; the violated taboo itself took vengeance. When at the later stage, ideas of Gods and spirits arose with whom taboo became associated, the penalty was expected to follow automatically from the divine power". (*Totem and Taboo*, P. 23) The above stated point is applicable to the first parents. They live in the Garden of Eden where God or the obsessional patient takes vengeance for eating forbidden fruit.

In the ancient days, people who committed this violation – either punished by the magical power or by the society itself, whose conduct caused their generation to reach a destructive peril. Thus in the ancient days the punishment for the violation of taboo was treated.

'Taboo' is a key concept which dominates the modern situation also. The human beings give much more reverence to the objects which are seen as something holy. The 'moral precepts and the codified laws are deeply rooted in the tabooed concepts. Though some human beings are rational beings in spirit, they are subjected to prohibitions – like moral, religious and social. In ancient days also the primitive people venerated the tabooed objects with a kind of awe but without asking question. There were number of prohibitions prevailed in the society but the people submit themselves to these prohibitions.

From here the course of this paper analyses the taboo committed in the Garden of Eden, and on whose responsibility this unwritten code of law is imposed in the Garden of Eden, where the first parents lived merrily. Christians are told that God is the Supreme Being in this world who created this world, and all know the story of the Genesis in the Bible. Here one has to keenly observe that God is zilch but a human being. Some may not accept this fact, but here the evidence proves that God is a man-like-man. "Then God said, "Let Us make man in Our image, according to Our likeness; let them have domination over ... all the earth and over every creeping thing that creeps on the earth." (Genesis, 1: 26). The Biblical line is changed by Milton in *Paradise Lost* book VII as:

Let us make now Man in our image, Man
In our similitude, and let the rule
Over the Fish and Fowl of Sea and Air,
Beast of the Field, and over all the Earth,
And every creeping thing that creeps the ground.
(519-523)

If one clearly notes the Miltonic line and one understands that even Milton, though he was a staunch Puritan, has given the emphasis that God is a man of man. God's words, in the previous lines, must be marked to show him as possessing human quality. So from now onwards the researcher writes the signifier God into god.

Let everyone remember the above said ideas from the Bible. So god is a human being and the human beings are the proof of it. But some say that he is a supreme being who reveals in every phenomenon and occurrence of nature, which are different kinds of issues. Since, god creates human in "His own image", he also has certain shortcomings in him.

Psychoanalytical field treats human being's life as a case study. Those who are obsessed with various individual prohibitions which are austerely observed by him in his private life, has been called an 'obsessional patient' – in other words 'taboo sickness' (Freud). The role of the Psychoanalytical field makes the hidden agenda to the visible world. A patient is created by various prohibitions in the society, so the irresistible fear is created in the patient who is abnormal. To them, there is someone who is always going against and warns. So finally "obsessional prohibitions involve just as extensive renunciations and restrictions in the loves of those who are subject to them." (*TT*, 33)

At this juncture, the researcher has arrived the right track at right time. The beginning of this article itself clearly states that this article is written only by following the literary masterpiece *Paradise Lost*. But here the researcher quotes from the Bible. One has to understand that Milton is a puritan and he has taken the material from the Bible since his purpose of writing the *Paradise Lost* is to "assert th' Eternal Providence, / And justifie the wayes of God to men" (Book I. Lines - 25-26). So the preference of the holy Bible instead of the "Paradise Lost" is a right choice to quote the exact sentence and the purpose of god in the Heaven.

The researcher argues that the god has the 'taboo sickness' in him. According to Freud, the primitive generations of people were sturdy believers in taboo. They created some rituals for worshipping the tabooed conception. They wanted some moral prohibitions to function the world properly. So without giving any meaning to the tabooed conception they blindly worshipped those prohibitions. God is the similar man who created this world within one week. He created almost all the things on the earth – starting from water to human beings.

But already this article has shown that those who have committed or violated the tabooed prohibitions let the way to fall the ceiling over the heads of their own generations of people. Adam and Eve are avenged by the tabooed concept in the Garden of Eden. Among the every created thing of god 'Forbidden fruit' or the 'tree of knowledge' is placed as something 'sacred' or 'uncanny'.

The god lets both Adam and Eve can have their rights 'over every living thing', of which the tree of knowledge needs some special perseverance. Psychoanalytical criticism believes that a person is obsessed with multi numbers of prohibitions, hence they are self-contradictory in nature. The strict observers of moral prohibitions are subjected to the abnormal condition, which is developed and strongly rooted in the childhood days of a man or woman. God has given rights to have an authority over everything in this world but the same man restricts Adam and Eve to taste the fruit of the knowledge. "God commanded the man, saying, "Of every tree of the Garden you may freely eat; but of the tree of the knowledge of good and evil you shall not eat," (*Genesis*, 16-17). Milton in Book VII writes these words of god from the Genesis as

This Garden, planted with the Trees of God,
Delectable both to behold and taste;
...... but of the Tree
Which tasted works knowledge of Good and Evil,
Thou may'st not; in the day eat'st, thou di'st;
Death is the penality impos'd, beware, (538 - 545)

The above mentioned line unveils the prevailed secrets of the unconscious realm of god. Since god is a man, he also has human wishes to be fulfilled. He has jealousy over both Adam and Eve, even though they are human beings. So he restricts them. For the generation of human beings, god is the first father who has laid down certain moral, social and uncodified prohibitions in the Garden of Eden. The successive generations have to follow those laws established by the previous generation. So they have to follow the tabooed desires of god.

The treacherous nature of god is unconcealed through the line that 'in the day that you eat of it [forbidden fruit] you shall surely die." (*Genesis*, 17) But this treachery is unveiled by the magical power or the demonic power called Satan. He says that when they eat the fruit from the tree of knowledge immediately their eyes will be opened. When the forbidden fruit is plucked and eaten by Eve, the act of renunciation compels God to prohibit Adam and Eve from the Heaven itself. He has the fear of losing his supremacy over his first generation of people. If their eyes are opened by the fruit from the 'tree of knowledge' some magical powers come to the human generation.

When god receives the shaking caused by both Adam and Eve, he has to prepare for the act renunciation since he is led by the obsessional prohibition. God has put forth the moral and uncodified laws for the 'tree of knowledge' and the fruits bore by it. Thus the conception of taboo is immediately imposed on the tree itself. That is the way Adam and Eve give their own veneration to the taboo – 'forbidden tree' – through the way of non-touching. Here what matters more is "Readiness is all" (*Hamlet*: Act V, Sc. II. 129) and "there is a special providence in the fall of" Adam and Eve.

God makes his mind to ready for the punishment. Here he renounces not the Garden of Eden but his own generation since he creates human beings with his own image. Adam is the replica of god but Eve is the replica of Adam, who makes clearance of Eve that "This is now bone of my bones / And flesh of my flesh; / She shall be called Woman," (23). Finally god's renunciation of his own 'hearts of hearts' are evicted from the Garden of Eden. The taboo sickness in god takes vengeance by saying that

"In the seat of your face you shall eat bread
Till you return to the ground,
For out of it you were taken;
For dust you are,
And dust you shall return." (G: 19)

God finally lets his unconscious mind to rule the world. The 'taboo sickness' finds its room in the unconscious realm of god. He, as an obsessional neurotic patient, 'willingly suspends' his own taboo sickness. So the mere sickness is 'loosed upon this world' as Yeats once believed that 'anarchy is loosed upon the world' ("The Second Coming").

Since Adam and Eve are the first parents in this world, let their generation at least may have the taboo-free society and prohibition-free society. But the modern world is already stainedbyT.S. Eliot. Once again the human beings are available to drag and lift up the same Sisyphean stone on their heads. This is what Existentialism taught the human beings. Since human beings have existential crisis, the unconscious portions of existence has the subconscious functions of the obsession and taboo sickness prohibitions in them.

The researcher argues that the era of God the Father (here he emphasizes the God) and his son Jesus Christ come to an end. Since human beings create god in their own exterior or vice-versa, may god be treated as a human being. The great writer of the early part of the Twentieth century, D. H. Lawrence, had conceived Jesus Christ as a Man who died in his novella *The Man Who Died.* He, in the tradition of Freud and his teachings, treats Jesus', as having the human qualities, subconscious thoughts. The researcher puts forth an idea that why can't god be treatedas having the human functions in him? The article proves that god as a human being with his own words as quoted in the *Genesis*. So both the Father and his Son can have human problems in them.

The paper does not aim to demolish the concept of god in this present scenario and at the same time it does not announce the author of this article as an atheist. The neutral position is observed throughout the composition. The objective of this article is to show that the present world is in great need of awareness over the environment of the present predicament of the human beings. If the article brings laurels let all of them go to Freud and his hardships, if it receives criticism let the blames go to the writer of this article as having an 'obsessional' prohibition.

Works Cited

1. Freud, Sigmund. *Totem and Taboo*. Trans. James Strachey. London and New York, Routledge Classics, 2001. Print.

2. Milton, John. *Paradise Lost*. New Delhi, UBSPD, 2015. Print.

3. Shakespeare. Williams. *Hamlet*. Edi. A. W. Verity. Cambridge University Press: London: 1989. Print.

4. *The Holy Bible*. New King James Version. Tennessee: Thomas Nelson Publishers, 1982. Print

CHAPTER V

'Cultural Hegemony' as Hegemonic Culture in Atwood's "The Handmaid's Tale"

The term 'Cultural Hegemony', one of the frequently mentioned terms in the Marxian theory, is elaborated in the *Prison Notebooks* of an Italian Marxist, namely, Antonio Gramsci, which denotes the cultural domination of the ruling class over the working class culture. Working class culture is slowly eroded by the culture of the bourgeoisie, whose power plays an important role in releasing Repressive State Apparatuses over powerless or working class people. According to Raymond Williams, a Welsh Socialist writer and cultural theorist, the word culture is an extremely difficult word to be defined. He defines it as a 'way of life'. Edward B. Tylor in his book *Primitive Culture* defines culture as a "complex whole which includes knowledge, belief, art, law, morals, custom, and any other capabilities and habits acquired by man as a member of society (*Primitive Culture*, 1).

Culture is an idea, it exists only in the minds of people. It is formulated for the surivival, hence, it is arbitrary in nature. The modern inventions are the products of culture. So one can say that it is a set of accepted beliefs, characters, collective behaviour, practices and the attitude of the society. Culture becomes hegemonic with the intrusion of the people. Power makes culture a hegemony over the people. It, with force, dominates the minds of the people for their acceptance and gradually replaces the former or already existing culture. So the hegemonical attitude of culture, because of power, imposes a new way of life into society.

The research statement of this paper denotes cultural hegemony as hegemonic culture in the novel *The Handmaid's Tale*. The difference between hegemonic culture and cultural hegemony is very simple. Cultural hegemony refers to the dominant culture where as hegemonic culture refers to the cultural domination of the dominated people. To impose the hegemonic culture in the society bourgeoisie uses Repressive State Apparatus.

Gramsci has pointed out, in *The Prison Notebooks*, the hegemo-centric attitude is prevailed through various 'Ideological State Apparatuses' (Althusser) like church, religion, government/state, and party. To implement its own authoritative ideologies (right-wing tendencies), among the people in the society, the State uses RSAs, in the extremists way/ Fascist methodologies, to make the people as 'interpellators'. The State uses the Repressive State Apparatuses, like police, institutions, and caste (in India) as a force to threaten people. This hegemo-centric attitude reigns in the novel *The Handmaid's Tale*. What Gramsci has said on religion is true in the novel. In it, the hegemonic attitude is carried out through RSAs.

The theme of the novel *The Handmaid's Tale* is drawn from The Old Testament. The story of the novel takes place somewhere in the future USA in the Republic of Gilead, a Christian land. The narrator is its lady protagonist, namely, Ofred, one of the handmaid's in the novel. The Republic of Gilead abolishes US constitution and has taken up the charge of ruling the Pre-Gilead people in USA. Gilead, as a State/Government, has laid down certain rigid conventions to be followed. It takes women in its custody and educates them to be the handmaids of the Commanders of the Republic of Gilead. Some of the Commanders, in the State, are known for their impotency. The widows, wives and other women in the pre-Gilead period are taken as the handmaids under the regime of the Republic of Gilead. If a handmaid is found to be infertile, she is sent to one of the colonies of Gilead, where they, however, lead the life of maids. Until the time of each handmaid comes to an end, she has to render her service to them. The handmaid's must wear red gown with full sleeve and a cap with a veil which hangs before their face. They are given a maid servant in the name of Marthas, who are without viable overies, act as the servants to the Commanders and the handmaids. If any one of the handmaids tries to escape from the Republic of Gilead, she is hanged publically, and the reason for their hanging is also hung with their carcass.

To subjugate the people the Republic of Gilead uses RSAs to get the consent of its own civil society. The RSAs in Gilead are considered Guardians of Faith, Eyes (Spy), the Wall, Angels (soldiers), Aunts and Colonies. With the help of these repressive systems, the Republic is functioning in USA. These repressive forces make the people to be subordinates of State. Atwood gives the pictorial condition of the Republic of Gilead through her narrator Ofred. In Gilead, "war cannot intrude except on television." (*The Handmaid's Tale*, 29) Gilead has no bounds. The doctors, lawyers and the students of the universities in the pre-Gilead is no longer the same in the land. The Universities are closed now. The studies have been put into a bound. The freedom of the people is restricted in the land. Women are not respected. The handmaid's are told that they are living in the happiest and in the free State. The Aunts, as one of the Repressive Apparatuses of Gilead, keep on advising the handmaids about the freedom given to handmaids.

The handmaids are not allowed to speak with other handmaids. They have not given a separate room. A Room of her own is banned here in the Republic. They sleep in the former US army cots. The Aunts, guarding them outside, have guns in their hands along with the Angels or soldiers. They are not permitted to enter into the place where the handmaids are sleeping, unless they are called for. On the whole the Republic of Gilead is a Police State.

The false ideology is given to the handmaids that their's "is a position of honour" (*The Handmaid's Tale*, 18). The commanders alone are supplied with wives and handmaids. Handmaids are respected in Gilead. They are not allowed to express their emotions, feelings and wishes towards other men, except Commanders. Ofred points out the position of men other than Commanders in Gilead. When the narrator and her Eyes Ofglen (spy), another handmaid who is assumed to be one of the spies of the State, walk for the shopping they produce their out passes to the soldiers, who should not whistle, touch and see the face of the handmaids. But Ofred lifts her veil to allow one of the soldiers, Nick, to see her face. Here she says the condition of the men in the State through the following lines.

As we walk away I know they're watching, these two men who aren't yet permitted to touch women. They touch with their eyes instead and I move my hips a little, feeling the red skirt sway around me. It's like thumbing your nose from behind a fence or teasing a dog with a bone held out of reach, I'm ashamed of myself for doing it, ... they're too young (28).

She continues that

Then I find I'm not ashamed after all. I enjoy the power; power of a dog bone, passive but there. ... They will suffer, later, at night in their regimented beds. They have no outlets now except themselves, and that's a sacrilege. There are no more magazines, no more films, no more substitutes; only me and my shadow, walking away from the two men, who ... watching our retreated shapes (28).

The Gramscian theorisation of the State/Government is applicable to the Republic of Gilead, which uses the cultural hegemony as to stamp its hegemonic ideologies among the civil society. A proper government/State, according to Gramsci, should establish a new type of law, which is "essentially innovatory". He also points out the significant role of the law to form a State. Thus he expresses that "If every State tends to create and maintain a certain type of civilisation and of citizen ..., and to eliminate certain customs and attitudes and to disseminate others, then the Law will be its instrument for this purpose" (*Selections from the Prison Notebooks*, 246). The State is an educator. It teaches civil society to become its subjects.

Gramsci believes that "[as] long as the class-State exists the regulated society cannot exist". The State in the novel is not at all a regulated government, rather it tries to regulate its own policies through RSAs. The prevalence of cultural hegemony in the State makes the ruling class to subject the subjects' collective consent. The use of the force, through the Angels, the Guardians of Faith and Aunts, help the State to spread its arms to get the consent of the handmaids (civil society) in the novel. Because of the fear towards the hanging in the public makes majority of the handmaids as interpellators. Hence, they are doubly marginalised in the Republic of Gilead.

The Republic of Gilead functions as an educator. It educates its handmaids how to adapt themselves to the newly formed culture. Women, as they reach the Republic of the Gilead, they are sent to the training centres namely, Rachel and Leah Centres. They have been educated and re-educated by the trainers in the centres.

Gramscian theorisation of the cultural hegemony revolves around two things, class and the State. There are two classes, the ruling class and subaltern class. The civil society is taken as the subaltern class. The nature of the subaltern class is determined by the ruling class. This ruling class forms the State, which is repressive, even representative too, apparatus of the Government. Gramsci has explained the conception of law and government by the religion. He once has pointed out that church and religion play a vital role to make the civil society as faithful subjects. The State is used as the major apparatus in two distinctive formats, the government and the 'private'. Under these private affairs comes religion and church. When it is in the hands of the private, it becomes the apparatus of 'hegemony' (261). Then there occurs the birth of "the dictatorial ideological current of the Right" (261).

When religion and the State/government combine together the type of dictatorial right-wing ideologies begin to dominate not only the culture but also the civilisation, civil society, and ethical society too. All institutions are known for their repressive treatment. Schools, medias, religion, and church are the major institutions through which the cultural domination takes place. In the Republic of Gilead too, both the religion and the State combine and form the fascist regime. In the fascist regime, writing, learning and thinking are prohibited. These fields are colonised and even commercialised. The customers become the one who are governed. Such is the status quo of the Republic of Gilead. It has closed the universities and Gramsci has rightly pointed out that "[w]here there is freedom, there is no State" (261).

Gramsci points out the limitation of the State, "whose functions are limited to the safeguarding of the public order and of respect for the laws" (261). But the Republic of Gilead fails in this aspect to protect its own people. It makes the position of women as a commodity. The Commanders, who are supplied with the handmaids, are consumers. The State Gilead functions as the Capitalists/bourgeoisie class. They reduce the respect of women to that of animals. They have fetched women as handmaids, and after removing their identity, they give them a new history. This is the extreme fascist movement which will be occurring not only in USA in near future but also in India too. Antonio Gramsci has already anticipated the situation in the early 1920s and 30s. The globalisation and other capitalistic notions will change the present world. This article is written after reading Gramsci's notion of the State and Government. The researcher has only applied the Marxist ideologies of both Gramsci and Althusser in the novel *The Handmaid's Tale*.

Works Cited

1. Althusser, Louis. "Ideology and Ideological State Apparatuses", *Lenin and Philosophy andOther Essays*. Trans. Ben Brewster. India: Aakar, 2006. Print.
2. Atwood, Margaret. *The Handmaid's Tale*. London: Vintage, 1996. Print.
3. Ferretter, Luke. *Louis Althusser*. London and New York: Routledge, 2006. Print.

4. Gramsci, Antonio. *Selections from the Prison Notebooks of Antonio Gramsci.* Edi. & trans. Quintin Hoare and Geoffrey Nowell Smith. India: Orient Longman, 1996. Print.

5. Jones, Steve. *Antonio Gramsci.* London and New York: Routledge, 2006. Print.

6. Tylor, Edward Birnett. *Primitive Culture.* New York: Dover Publications Inc, 1871. Print.

www.ingramcontent.com/pod-product-compliance
Lightning Source LLC
Chambersburg PA
CBHW051134160726
47997CB00019B/2511